BATTLE IN BAGHDAD

By Cory Gunderson

VISIT US AT
WWW.ABDOPUB.COM

Published by ABDO & Daughters, an imprint of ABDO Publishing Company, 4940 Viking Drive, Suite 622, Edina, Minnesota 55435.

Printed in the United States.

Edited by: Sheila Rivera
Contributing Editors: Chris Schafer, Paul Joseph
Graphic Design: Arturo Leyva, David Bullen
Cover Design: Castaneda Dunham, Inc.
Photos: AP/Wide World, Corbis, Department of Defense
Sources: *St. Paul Pioneer Press*, pages 12 and 13

Library of Congress Cataloging-in-Publication Data

Gunderson, Cory Gideon.
   Battle in Baghdad / Cory Gunderson.
     p. cm. -- (War in Iraq)
  Includes index.
  Summary: Describes events of the 2003 battle in Iraq's capital city, Baghdad, in which a coalition of nations led by the United States and Great Britain attempted to remove Saddam Hussein from power in order to set up a new government.
   ISBN 1-59197-494-1
  1. Iraq War, 2003--Juvenile literature. [1. Iraq War, 2003.] I. Title. II. Series

   DS79 .763.G86 2003
   956 .7044'3--dc22

2003052429

TABLE OF CONTENTS

Operation Iraqi Freedom begins with a bombing campaign.

COALITION GOALS

On March 19, 2003, a U.S.-led coalition launched a military campaign against the Iraqi government. This campaign was called Operation Iraqi Freedom. The battle in Baghdad would be only one conflict in the larger war. But many considered it the war's main battle.

U.S. military planners knew that Operation Iraqi Freedom could not be successful without conquering Baghdad. Baghdad is Iraq's capital. It is home to the country's government. Saddam Hussein was a longtime member of the Baath political party. He was Iraq's ruler for almost 25 years. He and many government leaders lived and worked in Baghdad.

Some United Nations (UN) members accused Saddam of possessing weapons of mass destruction. Over the years, the UN Security Council passed numerous UN resolutions aimed at ridding Iraq of these weapons. Sometimes Saddam complied with portions of the resolutions. Other times he disregarded them.

By 2002, U.S. president George W. Bush had grown tired of Saddam's defiance. Bush wanted to rid Iraq of these weapons. He was concerned that the weapons could be used

5

against U.S. citizens. He was also concerned about Saddam's ties to terrorists. Bush wanted to make sure that Saddam could not support terrorists who targeted U.S. interests. To do this, Bush wanted to make sure Saddam cooperated with the UN resolutions.

The UN is an organization made up of most countries in the world. Its goal is to keep peace in the world. It also seeks to bring security to all member nations. Terrorism and weapons of mass destruction threaten the world's peace and security. The UN knew that if Saddam had these weapons, they would be a threat to the world. For more than 12 years, the organization tried to force Saddam to comply with its resolutions. The UN resists using military force whenever possible. It preferred using diplomacy rather than military force to disarm Saddam.

Bush wanted Saddam to be held accountable for his lack of cooperation with the UN. He wanted the UN to authorize strict consequences for Saddam's defiance. Bush gained the support of British prime minister Tony Blair.

By late 2002, Bush and Blair began talking of military action against the Iraqi government. But the two leaders failed to gain UN support for that type of initiative. They decided to force Saddam to disarm Iraq without UN support. Bush and Blair built a military alliance of nations. It was called the Coalition of the Willing. Forty-seven nations banded together with the United States and United Kingdom against the Iraqi government.

U.S. president George W. Bush and British prime minister
Tony Blair vow to end Saddam Hussein's regime.

U.S. defense secretary Donald Rumsfeld identified the coalition's goals. One was to remove Saddam from power. Another goal was to find and destroy all Iraqi weapons of mass destruction. Coalition forces were to find any terrorists who had taken refuge in Iraq. Terrorists were to be captured or forced out of the country. The coalition also planned to help Iraq set up a new government. The new government would be designed differently than Saddam's. It was expected to cooperate with its neighbors.

The key to reaching the coalition's goals was to replace the Iraqi government. On March 17, 2003, Bush gave Saddam and his two sons 48 hours to leave Iraq. After they refused, the U.S.-led coalition began to bomb Iraq. There were battles in major Iraqi cities. All of them led up to the main battle in Baghdad. U.S. major general Victor Renuart summed up Baghdad's importance to the coalition forces. "Baghdad is really the heart of the regime [or Iraqi government], and I would expect it would hold its most valuable treasures close to its heart."

ANTICIPATING THE BATTLE

Months before the war on Iraq was declared, one of Saddam's leaders hinted at the dangers facing the soldiers who would fight in Baghdad. Mohammed Mehdi Saleh said, "Take the desert . . . If [coalition forces] want to change the political system in Iraq, they have to come to Baghdad. We will be waiting for them here."

Iraq had fought a U.S.-led coalition in 1991. That conflict was called the Persian Gulf War. Iraq had invaded Kuwait and taken control of it. Coalition forces went in to free Kuwait. The UN had supported the coalition's use of military force. It backed the coalition's freeing of Kuwait from Iraqi control.

During the Persian Gulf War, U.S.-led coalition forces killed thousands of Iraqi soldiers. There was little to cover the Iraqi soldiers in the desert. This made them easy targets for U.S. bombs and artillery. Iraq's military leaders would not make that same mistake again in 2003. Instead, they planned to lure coalition forces into the city of Baghdad.

Military combat within a heavily populated city is called urban warfare. Baghdad's population is more than 5 million. Its buildings are low and sprawl for miles. Iraqi leaders knew

that a battle in its capital city would be difficult for enemy forces. Concentrating Iraqi soldiers within the capital city would give Iraq advantages over its more powerful enemy.

Iraqi soldiers would have the advantage of being in a familiar area. They knew the city of Baghdad. The coalition forces would be in unfamiliar territory. The Iraqis could hide in any of the city's buildings and shoot at their enemy. They could use innocent Iraqi citizens to shield themselves from coalition forces.

To add to the coalition's challenge, not all Iraqi enemies would be dressed in military uniforms. It would be difficult for coalition forces to know which Iraqis were friends and which were foes.

A battle in Baghdad would offer the Iraqi military other advantages as well. Saddam knew that U.S. helicopters would have difficulty moving in a city. The Iraqi leader also knew that U.S. soldiers would not be able to carry heavy weapons into a city battle. The soldiers would need to pack lightly, so that they could move with ease. They would have to depend on small arms such as pistols. More powerful weapons would likely be too bulky.

Some coalition leaders feared Saddam might also launch a chemical attack against coalition soldiers. They worried that it would happen in Baghdad. Coalition soldiers would be slowed by having to fight in chemical weapons suits. These heavy suits had to be worn whenever the threat of chemical weapons existed. In the heat of Iraq, these suits could be as much of a hindrance as they were a help.

A U.S. soldier wearing a chemical weapons suit

GROUND TROOPS

How American soldiers fight and protect themselves

1 **HELMET**
- Kevlar helmet in desert camouflage colors
- Weighs 4 to 4.5 pounds (1.8 to 2 kg)

2 **GAS MASK**
- Valves in nose cup keep lenses from fogging; can be connected to filter canister or used alone

3 **CAMOUFLAGE CLOTHES**
- Color patches match colors of surroundings
- Irregular lines of color patches break up outline of soldier's shape
- Bare skin and shiny objects are covered
- For full benefit, soldiers move slowly

4 **MOLLE VEST** (Modular Lightweight Load Carrying Equipment)
- Three flap pockets each hold two 30-round magazines
- Two grenade pockets
- Two canteen pouches

5 **WEAPON**
- M16A1 rifle with a 30-round magazine and a 40mm M203 grenade launcher
- Fires a standard 5.56mm bullet
- Weighs 6.4 pounds (2.9 kg)

6 **NIGHT-VISION MOUNT**
- Allows soldiers to mount goggles that improve their ability to see at night

① ⑥ ③ ④ ⑤

READY FOR URBAN WARFARE

M2A3 Bradley Fighting Vehicle

Bradley Fighting Vehicles play an important role in urban warfare. U.S. soldiers practiced the following tactics to prepare themselves for such fighting.

- The Bradley reaches speeds of up to 45 mph (72 km/h) and carries infantry into battle. Just a few dozen yards from the enemy, the infantry get out of the vehicle.

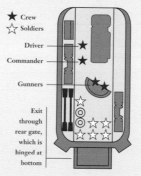

★ Crew
☆ Soldiers
Driver
Commander
Gunners
Exit through rear gate, which is hinged at bottom

- Four Bradleys make up a platoon. A platoon's vehicles arrive together at a certain location. Two squads of six soldiers get out of their Bradleys. They take cover behind the other two armored vehicles.

- The first two Bradleys remain in place. The second two Bradleys approach the targeted building slowly. The first two squads run alongside the Bradleys. They keep their eyes open for enemy troops.

- Once in position, the hatches on the last two Bradleys drop down. An additional 12 men run out. The platoon is ready to enter a building or walk down a narrow road that Bradley vehicles can't move down.

Saddam's government knew that fighting in Baghdad would likely result in the deaths of many coalition soldiers. It would also cause many civilian deaths. The Iraqi government could use a high death count to its advantage. It would blame the deaths of innocent people on the invading forces. The deaths of coalition soldiers, as well as civilians, might cause the U.S.-led forces to rethink their invasion. Saddam would do all he could to weaken the coalition's resolve.

The U.S. military believed that Saddam might set up military operations in hospitals and mosques in the cities. He was known to have used both to his political advantage before. He knew what would happen if the United States bombed an Iraqi hospital or mosque. World opinion would condemn it.

Retired U.S. general John Hoar said there was no doubt the coalition forces would defeat Saddam's government. His concern was that the world would watch "while we win and have military rounds exploding in [heavily] populated Iraqi neighborhoods."

U.S. military planners knew the dangers of urban warfare. U.S. troops had been involved in urban warfare during conflicts in other countries. The planners were also aware of trenches Saddam's workers had dug around Baghdad. They suspected Saddam would have the trenches filled with oil, and then have the oil set on fire. The oily smoke would lessen the effectiveness of U.S. guidance systems, which are used to direct weapons to their targets. Saddam had ordered the burning of many oil wells in Kuwait during the Persian Gulf War. He was not above such destruction.

Military planners tried to avoid urban warfare whenever possible. Past experience made some experts predict that one in three soldiers could die fighting in the cities of Iraq. However, the planners knew that to remove Saddam from power, urban warfare would likely be necessary.

U.S. military leaders worked to reduce the Iraqi advantage in the anticipated urban warfare. U.S. troops prepared for what likely awaited them in the streets of Baghdad and other Iraqi cities. About 18,000 soldiers were trained in urban warfare. They practiced fighting in mock cities set up in military forts. Soldiers learned to use ropes to climb onto enemy rooftops. They learned how to navigate at night and how to storm buildings.

Coalition leaders hoped to weaken Saddam's government and military before their troops got to Baghdad. The launch of a massive air assault would help. It would pave the way for ground troops to enter Iraq's capital city. The plan was to lessen Iraqi resistance under the assault. The coalition wanted the Iraqis to be more afraid of further coalition assaults than they were of disobeying Saddam.

Coalition leaders also hoped that Iraqi citizens and soldiers would rise up against Saddam. An Iraqi revolt against Saddam would make his removal from power easier. It would also spare both sides the devastation of urban warfare in Baghdad. Fewer Iraqis and coalition troops would die. A revolt would also reduce the amount of construction needed to rebuild Iraq after the war.

IRAQ'S LEADERS

Saddam Hussein

Before Saddam's rise to power, he attempted to assassinate Iraqi prime minister Abdul Kassem. Saddam was forced to flee Iraq.

When the Baath party gained control of Iraq in 1963, Saddam returned to the country and rejoined the party.

Saddam held positions within the Baath party, such as assistant secretary general, vice chairman of the Revolutionary Command Council, and vice president.

Saddam became president of Iraq in 1979 and held this position until Operation Iraqi Freedom removed him from power.

Uday Hussein

Uday is Saddam's eldest son.

Many thought he would lead Iraq after Saddam. An assassination attempt on his life in 1996 left him severely wounded. After this, he seemed less likely to succeed his father.

Uday was a National Assembly member.

He served as chairman of Iraq's Olympic committee.

He was also chief of the Saddam Feyadeen soldiers.

Uday controlled Iraq's media, including the country's most popular newspaper and a popular television channel for Iraqi youth.

Qusay Hussein

Qusay is Saddam's second oldest son.

Many believed Saddam was grooming him to be Iraq's next leader.

He supervised Iraq's Republican Guard.

Qusay was responsible for Saddam's personal security.

He was also put in charge of defending Baghdad and Tikrit during the U.S.-led coalition attack against Iraq in 2003.

AIR ASSAULT ON BAGHDAD

From the beginning of Operation Iraqi Freedom on March 19, bombs lit the night sky over Baghdad. The first ones targeted Saddam and his sons, Uday and Qusay, in southern Baghdad. Military officials had told President Bush that they had information that placed Saddam and his sons in a bunker there. Saddam had underground bunkers built to protect him from enemy attack. The officials believed that other Iraqi leaders were in the same location.

Two EGBU-27 bombs weighing 2,000 pounds (907 kg) each were directed to hit Saddam's bunker. These laser-guided bombs are so precise that they can come within 3 feet (1 m) of their targets. Coalition leaders hoped that the bombing would kill Saddam.

This initial attack was part of the coalition's decapitation strategy. To decapitate something is to remove its head. The coalition strategy intended to remove the "head" of the Iraqi government. Saddam, his sons, and other government leaders made up that head. Coalition forces hoped that Saddam's death early in the conflict would result in a shorter war with fewer deaths.

The results of the coalition's first air strikes are visible in Baghdad.

Even if Saddam lived through the attack, the coalition wanted to make it difficult for him to communicate with his military. It wanted to reduce Saddam's ability to control any part of the conflict. Coalition forces did not know whether Saddam had survived the attack. Until they knew for certain, they had to operate as if he was still alive.

U.S. planes dropped more bombs and missiles on military targets in central Baghdad. Iraq's capital shook with explosions. Saddam's family home was among the buildings hit. U.S. secretary of defense Donald Rumsfeld explained the bombing attacks in and around Baghdad. "What will follow will not be a repeat of any other conflict. It will be of a force and scope and scale that has been beyond what has been seen before."

On March 21, U.S. ground forces seized partial control of Umm Qasr. This is an important Iraqi port city. Control of Umm Qasr provided coalition forces a route to move supplies from the Persian Gulf into Iraq. Coalition troops secured oil fields west of Basra. Their job was to keep Iraqis from setting the fields on fire.

Meanwhile, Baghdad faced its third night of air strikes. These strikes and later ones were part of a campaign to "shock and awe" the Iraqi military. The U.S. military hoped that the strikes would cause the Iraqi people to surrender to the coalition.

Coalition forces on the ground advanced toward Baghdad. But they suffered setbacks in other parts of Iraq. On March 23, Iraqi forces ambushed 15 members of the 507th Ordnance Maintenance Company near An Nasiriya. The group of U.S.

military vehicles was traveling in south-central Iraq. The vehicles had made a wrong turn. Two Iraqi tanks and a group of Iraqi soldiers confronted them. Five soldiers from the 507th were captured. Eight others, including Jessica Lynch, were listed as missing in action. Two soldiers were confirmed dead.

The five captives became prisoners of war (POWs). Arab broadcast network al-Jazeera displayed images of the POWs on television. The bodies of dead U.S. soldiers were also displayed. By showing the POWs on television, the Iraqi government violated the Geneva convention. This series of agreements was first written at an international convention in Geneva, Switzerland, in 1864. The Geneva convention outlines rules of war and the proper treatment of POWs. Leaders from around the world agreed to treat prisoners of war according to this agreement. Coalition leaders condemned the al-Jazeera broadcast, saying it showed disrespect in displaying the images.

By March 24, the bombing in Baghdad was aimed at Republican Guard bunkers that circled the city. The Republican Guard was made up of Saddam's best-trained and most well equipped soldiers. Coalition leaders wanted to weaken the guard's ability to fight coalition forces. The bombing battered Iraqi positions and damaged Iraq's defense. Some coalition ground soldiers were now just 50 miles (80 km) south of Baghdad.

Coalition ground forces continued battling Iraqi forces in Umm Qasr. They attacked the cities of Basra and An Najaf as well. Meanwhile, U.S. forces bombed Republican Guard

Iraqi Republican Guard bunkers in Baghdad come under attack by coalition forces.

camps in southern Baghdad. U.S. forces hoped that this bombing would further weaken the Iraqis' defense of their capital. Weakened Iraqi defenses would pose less of a threat to coalition ground forces. Coalition leaders also wanted to spare the ground troops the threat of chemical attacks that could be launched by the Republican Guard.

Air raids on Baghdad continued even as fighting slowed U.S. ground forces. On March 29, four U.S. soldiers were stationed at a military inspection point near An Najaf. An Iraqi man in a taxi waved for help. He was a suicide bomber, but the soldiers did not know it. As they approached the cab, the Iraqi man set off explosives. The man and the soldiers died.

On April 1, Iraq's Olympic headquarters was hit in air attacks. An air force officers' club was also struck. Saudi Arabian leaders urged Saddam to leave Iraq. They suggested he bring the war to an end. Coalition forces were still not certain whether Saddam was dead or alive.

By April 2, U.S. ground forces were only 19 miles (31 km) from Baghdad. Bombing of the capital continued. Coalition forces wanted to destroy the Iraqi government's ability to plan and communicate its military strategy.

THE GROUND INVASION

Coalition leaders had set their sights on Baghdad from the beginning of Operation Iraqi Freedom. In early April, one military official said, "The goal is to punch here, punch there and then go get [Baghdad]." Coalition forces had gotten in their punches in cities across Iraq. It appeared as though the focus of the ground war was about to shift. Coalition air raids had paved the way for ground troops to invade and conquer Baghdad.

Just days before coalition ground troops entered Baghdad, the U.S. military made a daring rescue. An Iraqi lawyer named Mohammed al-Rehaief had contacted the U.S. military. He told military personnel that a wounded U.S. soldier was in the Saddam Hospital in An Nasiriya. He had seen the female soldier when he visited his wife, who worked in the hospital as a nurse. The man was concerned for the soldier's safety.

On April 2, a team of U.S. Navy SEALs forced its way into the hospital. Outside, Army Rangers provided security. Marines created noise nearby. Their goal was to call attention away from the rescue mission. U.S. Air Force Special Operations Command had a helicopter waiting. It would

Ground troops push farther into Iraq to prepare for the ground invasion.

transport the soldier to freedom and safety. The mission was a success. The soldiers rescued nineteen-year-old Private First Class Jessica Lynch. She was one of the soldiers listed as missing in action since March 23.

By the next day, about 1,000 U.S. soldiers from the Third Infantry Division reached Saddam International Airport. The airport is located 10 miles (16 km) from the center of Baghdad. The soldiers' arrival followed a heavy air raid on the airport. After fighting Iraqi resistance, coalition forces seized control of it.

Also on April 3, coalition bombing knocked out Baghdad's electricity. Some believed this was done to pave the way into a darkened Baghdad for coalition special forces. The lack of electricity would help coalition forces move into Baghdad more safely. Iraqi soldiers would not be able to see them as easily in total darkness.

The lack of electricity made life difficult for Baghdad's citizens. Without electricity, water treatment facilities couldn't clean drinking water. Without clean drinking water, health problems can result. In some areas of Baghdad, no drinking water was available.

At a news briefing that day, U.S. brigadier general Vincent Brooks described the coalition's progress. He said, "The dagger is clearly pointed at the heart of the regime." Sergeant Jeff Lanter described the coalition position in a different way. He said, "The noose is starting to tighten around Baghdad."

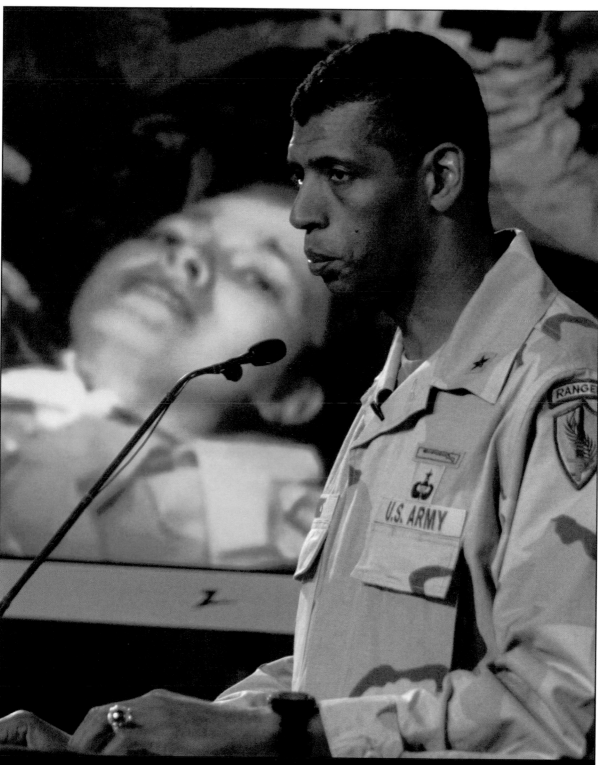

Brigadier General Vincent Brooks speaks during a news conference. An image of the rescued Jessica Lynch is behind him.

To keep the airport under coalition control, hundreds of U.S. soldiers were flown in on April 4. Their job was to help keep it from Iraqi forces. Lieutenant Colonel Woody Radcliffe called the struggle for the airport "the biggest fight of the war." U.S. forces renamed the airport Baghdad International. Removing Saddam's name from the airport was one more blow to his power.

Someone said to be Saddam was shown on Iraqi television that same day. The man walked around greeting Iraqis on the streets of Baghdad. Coalition forces did not know if it was really Saddam. They questioned whether it was someone else made to look like him.

Around the country, many Iraqi soldiers dropped their weapons. They fled from coalition forces. Up to 400 Iraqi soldiers were said to have surrendered at one time. It was reported that some had changed into street clothing. They ran off, leaving their uniforms and weapons behind them.

Coalition tanks ventured into a Baghdad suburb on April 5. This display of military power allowed coalition forces to see what Iraqi resistance remained. U.S. secretary of state Colin Powell declared that day, "We're almost in control of their country and we'll be in complete control soon."

As coalition forces neared Baghdad, hundreds of Iraqis left the capital. An Iraqi official threatened more suicide bombings by Iraqi citizens. Two female suicide bombers killed themselves and three U.S. soldiers with a car bomb. After the bombing in western Iraq, al-Jazeera broadcast a video on television. The

video showed two women claiming to be suicide bombers. The women told of their willingness to die for Saddam's government. The tape was claimed to have been recorded earlier by the two women who had died. More suicide attacks followed.

A man who looked like Saddam appeared on television again. He told Baghdad citizens to strike out against the coalition forces. Instead, thousands of citizens packed up what they could and headed for safety. Massive traffic jams resulted as residents poured out of Baghdad.

On April 6, British troops destroyed Baath party headquarters in Basra. This was another blow to Saddam's regime, because he had been a longtime Baath party member. That same day, U.S. troops closed off main roads into Baghdad. Air strikes on the capital continued.

The next day, coalition forces made significant strikes against Saddam's regime. They destroyed two of his palaces. Meanwhile, U.S. Marines enjoyed the lavish palaces that had not been destroyed. They took showers in the palace bathrooms and sat on expensive furniture. Photos of them in the palaces were taken and published widely. U.S. forces also blew up a statue of Saddam on horseback in the center of the city.

In a wealthy part of Baghdad called Mansour, coalition forces bombed three houses. They destroyed the site where Saddam and his sons were thought to be meeting. U.S. officials were unable to confirm whether Saddam and his sons were there.

THE FALL OF SADDAM

U.S. troops use a tank to topple a statue of Saddam Hussein in Baghdad.

Saddam's control of Baghdad appeared to come to an end by April 9. U.S. Marines and crowds of Iraqis toppled a large statue of Saddam. It had sat in the center of the capital. News footage showed Iraqi citizens dragging the head of the statue through the streets. Some Iraqis pounded it with their shoes. They did this to show their disrespect for Saddam. The U.S. base of operations declared that Iraq had reached the "tipping point." Saddam's rule had come to an end.

White House spokesman Ari Fleischer reacted to the celebration in Baghdad's streets. He said, "Freedom's taste is unquenchable. You're seeing what you see in mankind everywhere, given a chance to be free."

BAGHDAD OUT OF CONTROL

The end of Saddam's regime raised not only cheers in the streets of Baghdad. It also brought lawlessness and looting. There was no government left to control the Iraqi people. Some took advantage of the situation.

CBS News reporter Byron Pitts was in Iraq's capital. He witnessed what happened in the city without a government. On April 8, 2003, he wrote: " . . . On the bombed and broken streets of East Baghdad, 'freedom' meant free. Free TVs, VCRs, computers, and air conditioners. There was even a bashful shopper with an armful of stolen AK-47s. If a man, woman, or child could carry it, it was theirs."

U.S. Marines patrolled the streets of Baghdad. Initially, they did not arrest those who stole. Some who witnessed the wrongdoing understood what drove the looters. The looters were Iraqi citizens who had watched for years as Saddam enjoyed luxuries they were denied. Now was their chance. They took what once belonged exclusively to Saddam and members of the Baath party.

Coalition leaders were somewhat concerned about the lack of order and the lawlessness in Baghdad. They counted

Iraqi citizens view the damage to one of Saddam's palaces after it was looted.

on being able to eventually restore order. Brigadier General Brooks attended a military briefing on April 9. He offered his view of the situation. He said, "I think in this case we're seeing a lot of jubilation and people who have long been oppressed for years and years having choices. We believe that this will settle down in due time."

Unfortunately, before the looting could be stopped, the Iraq National Museum in Baghdad fell victim. This museum displayed Iraq's greatest treasures of ancient history. Thousands of pieces represented civilizations from thousands of years earlier. Some were from ancient Mesopotamia. All were precious and irreplaceable.

Ancient funeral masks and jeweled musical instruments were stolen. Clay tablets, coins, and priceless jewelry were also taken. Left behind were shattered display cases and broken pottery bowls. Abdul Rakhman was the museum's live-in guard. He told reporters that he heard some looters say that there was no government and that everything belonged to them.

Ali Mahmoud, another museum employee, shared his frustration. He regretted the destruction of billions of dollars worth of valuables. He said, "This is the property of this nation and the treasure of 7,000 years of civilization. What does this country think it is doing?"

Some blamed the United States for the country's loss. Iraq's antiquities chief, Jabar Hilil, was one of them. He said, "If the American forces had been here, nothing would have happened . . . but it seems they had other priorities than the

museum." U.S. officials said the plundering of the museum surprised them. They said that U.S. troops had been engaged in combat and unable to prevent the museum looting.

People around the world reacted to the looting of the museum. Islamic *imams*, or prayer leaders, urged looters to return the stolen treasures. Members of a White House cultural advisory committee resigned their positions to protest the loss of Iraqi treasures. They were disappointed that the U.S. military had failed to protect the museum. Investigators from outside Iraq promised to help find and return the objects that were stolen. Some speculated that professional thieves did some of the looting.

While many Iraqis cheered Saddam's downfall, they depended on the U.S. and coalition forces to keep order. Up through the first part of April, U.S. military commander Tommy Franks had only promised to protect the foundation of Iraq's government. He had not promised that the coalition would protect other buildings such as the museum.

On April 12, the military changed its position. It announced that Iraqi police and U.S. Marines would work together. Jointly, they would patrol Baghdad to keep it safe. To help gain order in the city, a curfew was also established. Within a couple of days, some reporters noted that Iraqi police and U.S. patrols were visible. Order was beginning to return to the streets of Baghdad.

Former POW Shoshana Johnson after her rescue

FROM BAGHDAD TO TIKRIT

After the fall of Baghdad, some coalition forces headed toward Tikrit. Tikrit was Saddam's hometown, and many of his supporters still lived there. Through the years, Saddam had granted favors to some people in his home city. Tikrit was the only significant Iraqi city not yet controlled by the coalition.

As U.S. Marines moved toward Tikrit on April 13, an Iraqi man stopped them. He said that they would soon "come into contact with a number of Americans." His words proved true. The marines found and rescued seven POWs in Samarra. Samarra is located about 35 miles (56 km) south of Tikrit. All the POWs were in good physical shape, though two of the seven soldiers had gunshot wounds.

Five of the rescued soldiers—Specialist Edgar Hernandez, Specialist Joseph Hudson, Specialist Shoshana Johnson, Private First Class Patrick Miller, and Sergeant James Riley—were from the 507th Maintenance Company. Jessica Lynch belonged to the same company. These soldiers were part of the convoy that had been ambushed near An Nasiriya on March 23.

The other two rescued that day were Chief Warrant Officer David S. Williams and Chief Warrant Officer

From left to right: former POWs Specialist Edgar Hernandez, Private First Class Patrick Miller, Sergeant James Riley, and Specialist Joseph Hudson

Ronald D. Young. Both men were part of the First Battalion of the 227th Aviation Regiment. Iraqi officials had claimed earlier that on March 23 Iraqi farmers shot down the Apache helicopter the soldiers were in. Coalition leaders did not believe Iraqi farmers were responsible for bringing down the Apache.

All seven of the rescued soldiers were flown to Kuwait for medical help. After their release, they climbed out of helicopters to a joyful welcome from troops at an airbase in southern Iraq.

Meanwhile, U.S. ground forces continued to push ahead to Tikrit. Previous U.S. air strikes had weakened the city's military power. Still, a convoy of television vehicles came under fire as it entered the center of the city on April 13. But by the next day, Tikrit had fallen to coalition forces. The last major Baath party stronghold was defeated.

The fall of Tikrit marked the end of combat in the war against Iraq. At this point, instead of working to seize key pieces of Iraqi land, U.S. forces targeted pockets of Iraqi resistance. They also shifted their priorities to rebuilding Iraq and to the establishment of a new Iraqi government.

In order to help Iraq build a new government, the U.S. military had to make sure Saddam's government was completely removed from power. Some former Iraqi officials had been killed or captured. Many were unaccounted for. Those whose location and status were unknown posed a threat to the future of the new government. Coalition forces

Iraqi citizens celebrate near the U.S. Apache helicopter that David S. Williams and Ronald D. Young were piloting before it was shot down.

could not count on these officials to leave their powerful positions without a fight.

To help U.S. forces find these "most wanted" officials, U.S. military personnel designed a deck of playing cards. Each card displayed the face, title, and name of a former Iraqi regime leader. The aces, kings, queens, and jacks were the highest-ranking Iraqi officials. They were most wanted by the U.S. government. Next in ranking were Iraqi military leaders. National ministers and advisers ranked next. Less powerful regional Iraqi officials appeared on the lowest cards. The decks of cards were given to U.S. soldiers in Iraq. This deck was to help U.S. forces identify and capture former government officials.

On May 1, 2003, President Bush declared that combat operations in Iraq were finished. However, much to the coalition's disappointment, the most wanted Iraqis were unaccounted for. Saddam, Uday, and Qusay, the aces of spades, hearts, and clubs, were still missing.

The conflict in Baghdad had either driven Saddam and his sons into hiding or had left them buried in rubble. Though the battle in Baghdad was a victory, the mystery of Saddam and his sons' fate remained even after the war ended.

WEB SITES
WWW.ABDOPUB.COM

To learn more about the battle in Baghdad, visit ABDO Publishing Company on the World Wide Web at **www.abdopub.com**. Web sites about the battle are featured on our Book Links page. These links are routinely monitored and updated to provide the most current information available.

An Iraqi man stands in the rubble of his house in Baghdad.

TIMELINE

1991
Persian Gulf War

MARCH 17, 2003
President Bush gave Saddam 48 hours to leave Iraq

MARCH 19, 2003
U.S.–led coalition began attack against Iraq

MARCH 23, 2003
Members of the 507th Ordnance Maintenance Company ambushed
near An Nasiriya

APRIL 1, 2003
Iraq's Olympic headquarters hit in air attacks

APRIL 2, 2003
POW Private First Class Jessica Lynch rescued by U.S. Special Forces

APRIL 3, 2003
Coalition forces seized control of Saddam International Airport

APRIL 5, 2003

Coalition tanks ventured into a Baghdad suburb for first time since war began

APRIL 6, 2003

Baath party headquarters in Basra destroyed by British forces

APRIL 9, 2003

Baghdad no longer under Saddam's control

APRIL 10, 2003

Iraq National Museum in Baghdad looted

APRIL 13, 2003

Seven POWs rescued outside Samarra

APRIL 14, 2003

Tikrit fell to coalition forces

MAY 1, 2003

President Bush declared that combat operations in Iraq were finished

FAST FACTS

- Saddam Hussein led Iraq for nearly 25 years.

- Baghdad is Iraq's capital and home to the country's government.

- Many world leaders regarded Saddam as a threat to world peace. Not all could agree on how to eliminate this threat.

- The United Nations (UN) tried for more than 12 years to get Saddam to disarm.

- The U.S.-led coalition did not have UN support for its invasion of Iraq.

- British prime minister Tony Blair was President Bush's strongest supporter in the coalition's invasion of Iraq.

- U.S. leaders were concerned about the possibility of urban warfare in Baghdad. About 18,000 U.S. troops were trained to fight within the cities of Iraq.

- After U.S. forces seized control of Saddam International Airport, they renamed it Baghdad International.

- Tikrit is Saddam's hometown and the last significant Iraqi city to fall to the coalition forces.

- U.S. soldiers were given a deck of cards. The cards displayed photos of Iraqi officials who were most wanted by the U.S. government. This deck was to help U.S. soldiers identify and capture former government officials.

GLOSSARY

Air Force Special Operations Command:
A unit of the U.S. Air Force whose members are organized, trained, and equipped to conduct special, secret operations to achieve military objectives.

AK-47:
An assault rifle.

antiquities:
Items from ancient times, especially before the Middle Ages.

Army Rangers:
A unit of the U.S. Army whose members are organized, trained, and equipped to conduct special, secret operations to achieve military objectives.

artillery:
Large weapons that are operated by military crews.

convoy:
A group of motor vehicles that travel together.

jubilation:
An expression of joy.

mosque:
A Muslim place of worship.

network:
A company that produces programs for a chain of broadcasting stations.

noose:
A loop of rope that gets tighter as it's pulled.

SEALs:
A unit of the U.S. Navy whose members are organized, trained, and equipped to conduct special, secret operations to achieve military objectives.

weapons of mass destruction (WMD):
Weapons that kill or injure large numbers of people, or cause massive damage to buildings. When people talk about weapons of mass destruction, they are usually referring to nuclear, biological, or chemical weapons.

INDEX